2021
BUENOS AIRES

Restaurants

The Food Enthusiast's Long Weekend Guide

Andrew Delaplaine

GET 3 FREE NOVELS
Like political thrillers?
See next page to download 3 FREE page-turning novels—no strings attached.

Andrew Delaplaine *is the Food Enthusiast.*
When he's not playing tennis,
he dines anonymously at the Publisher's (considerable)
expense.

WANT 3 FREE THRILLERS?

Why, of course you do!
If you like these writers--
Vince Flynn, Brad Thor, Tom Clancy, James Patterson, David Baldacci, John Grisham, Brad Meltzer, Daniel Silva, Don DeLillo
If you like these TV series –
House of Cards, Scandal, West Wing, The Good Wife, Madam Secretary, Designated Survivor

---

You'll love the **unputdownable** series about Jack Houston St. Clair, with political intrigue, romance, and loads of action and suspense.

Besides writing travel books, I've written political thrillers for many years that have delighted hundreds of thousands of readers. I want to introduce you to my work!
Send me an email and I'll send you a link where you can download the first 3 books in my bestselling series, absolutely FREE.

Mention **this book** when you email me.
andrewdelaplaine@mac.com

Copyright © by Gramercy Park Press - All rights reserved.
Cover photo by Axel Eres on Unsplash

The Food Enthusiast's Long Weekend Guide

Table of Contents

INTRODUCTION – 5

THE A TO Z LISTINGS – 11
*Ridiculously Extravagant
Sensible Alternatives
Quality Bargain Spots*

NIGHTLIFE – 57

Index – 65
(includes Cuisine Index)

Other Books by the Food Enthusiast – 68

Introduction

DID YOU FIND AN INTERESTING PLACE?
If you discover a place you think I should check out on my next visit, drop me a line, will you? I'll mention your name if I end up listing it.
andrewdelaplaine@mac.com

What a fascinating country. You walk down the avenues of BA and look at some of the well-heeled ladies and gentlemen promenading and you'd never know the country is always on the brink of some new disaster (usually self-inflicted), whether it's a debt crisis, or a political scandal involving some important person's assassination. Whatever it is, it's always something.

But somehow BA not only endures, it thrives. There's a sophistication about the people here that manages to transcend the ephemeral problems that besiege the country as a whole.

It's always reminded me of Marseille, that other polyglot of a town. In Marseille, because it was such a centrally located trading port, there's the confluence of cultural influences that go back 3,000 years—all surging together in that remarkable city.

Here in BA, the Romans never landed and the Carthaginians never tramped through on their elephants, but still BA has an impressive mixture of cultural elements from France, Spain, Portugal, Italy—everywhere, really.

These bedazzling influences have combined to create a vibrant dining scene that has become even more impressive in the last few years.

Get ready for an onslaught of meat-based dishes. The Atkins diet on steroids. Nobody handles meat the way these guys do. (That reminds me of something Sarah Palin said: "If God hadn't wanted us to eat animals, He wouldn't have made them out of meat.")

So, between your tango lessons and visits to what has to be one of the most interesting cemeteries in the world (the Recoleta), spend as much time as you can in the eateries of Buenos Aires.

You will agree with native son Jorge Luis Borges, that, "To me, it seems a mere tale that Buenos Aires had a beginning: I judge her to be as eternal as water and air."

A WORD ABOUT MONEY
The official exchange rate is a joke, so both locals and tourists have turned to the black market to get what they call "blue dollars." *Arbolitos* are street hawkers who help you get these blue dollars. You will hear them yelling "Cambio!" Hook up with one of them and they will take you to *Cuevas* that sell currency. A site giving you the current rate is www.lanacion.com -- this can save you a lot of money.

The A to Z Listings

Ridiculously Extravagant
Sensible Alternatives
Quality Bargain Spots

DID YOU FIND AN INTERESTING PLACE?
If you discover a place you think I should check out on my next visit, drop me a line, will you? I'll mention your name if I end up listing it.
andrewdelaplaine@mac.com

A note on the **Puertas Cerradas** (or "closed door" restaurants) that abound in BA. They don't like to give out their addresses as a rule until you get a reservation from them. Try emailing first, then calling. Much better if you get someone who speaks Spanish to do it for you. But these are great spots and very much worth the effort.)

ACONCAGUA
Bolívar 905, Buenos Aires, +54 11 4362-3826
CUISINE: Argentinean
DRINKS: Full bar
SERVING: Breakfast, Lunch & Dinner; closed Sun
PRICE RANGE: $
NEIGHBORHOOD: San Telmo
A classic old bar located in a quiet corner of San Telmo populated by locals. Great menu of homemade cuisine, all cooked when you order it. They have daily set menus, and this is what you want to try. Open 24 hours a day. On Sundays the locals gather to watch sports.

ALDO'S VINOTECA
Moreno 372 Caba, Buenos Aires, 54 11 4334-2380
www.aldosvinoteca.com
CUISINE: Argentinean

DRINKS: Full Bar
SERVING: Breakfast, Brunch, Late night
PRICE RANGE: $$
NEIGHBORHOOD: Monserrat; San Telmo
Located in the heart of the city in the **Moreno Hotel,** this restaurant offers and elegant dining experience. Nice menu and perhaps the most impressive wine list in town (over 40 pages) with mostly Argentine wines but some Spanish and Italian labels. Nice choice for Sunday brunch.

ARAMBURU
Salta 1050 Caba, Buenos Aires, +54 11 4305-0439
www.arambururesto.com.ar
CUISINE: Argentinian/International
DRINKS: Full Bar
SERVING: Dinner
PRICE RANGE: $$$$
NEIGHBORHOOD: Constitucion
Raw brick walls greet you as you enter. The eye drifts to the clear glass window that lets you look into the kitchen. Known as one of the top five restaurants in Buenos Aires and like most of the finer restaurants a reservation is a must. The menu is in courses (last time I was there we had 16 courses all paired with wine for less than $100) but they offer many delicious dishes like White Salmon and Filet Mignon. Great selection of wines. If they are jammed (and they usually are), opt for the less formal place across the street, **Aramburu Bis**, owned by the same chef. After dinner, check out the bar downstairs in the basement.

BOULEVARD SAENZ PENA
Saenz Pena 1400, Buenos Aires, 54 11 5197 4776
www.boulevardsaenzpena.com.ar/
CUISINE: Argentinian
DRINKS: Full Bar
SERVING: Breakfast, Lunch, Dinner
PRICE RANGE: $$$$

NEIGHBORHOOD: Capital Federal
This unique eatery offers a pre-fix menu by Chef Juliana Lopez May, one of the top chefs in Argentina. This place also sells art, antiques, and gifts, so it's a lot more than a restaurant. It's like a shop that serves excellent food. (You can even buy the plate you eat from.) Menu favorites include: Pasta with Butternut Squash and Rucola Salad with pear and blue cheese.

CAFÉ LA BIELA
Avenida Quintana 600, Buenos Aires, 54 11 4804-0449
www.labiela.com
CUISINE: Cafeteria
DRINKS: Full Bar
SERVING: Lunch, Dinner
PRICE RANGE: $$$
NEIGHBORHOOD: Recoleta
This traditional Argentine café, originally a meeting place for racecar drivers, is one of the oldest cafés in BA, going back 150 years. You'll see the walls inside this place lined with racecar memorabilia, lots of photos of famous drivers—most now long dead—look down from the walls. Though it's a bit of a tourist trap in the way Sloppy Joe's is in Key West, it's still worth visiting. I prefer inside where you get the dark wood paneling, the ceiling fans and the charm. I don't fancy the plastic chairs outside, but in good weather it's a really nice spot. Extensive menu

serving large portions. Jorge Luis Borges, probab;ly the m,ost famous writer NOT awarded the Nobel Prize, lived just a short walk from here, and used to visit often.

CASA FELIX
Address given with reservation, 54 9 11 4555-1882

www.colectivofelix.com
CUISINE: Argentinean
DRINKS: Full Bar
SERVING: Dinner
PRICE RANGE: $$$$
NEIGHBORHOOD: El Centro
Closed Door Restaurant. This place only seats 12 guests for a private five-course tasting menu three times a week. Menu changes with each seating but the dishes are creative and tasty. Long wait for reservations.

CAFÉ SAN JUAN
Chile 474, Buenos Aires, 54 11 4300-9344
No Website
CUISINE: Italian/Spanish
DRINKS: Full Bar
SERVING: Breakfast, Lunch, Dinner
PRICE RANGE: $
NEIGHBORHOOD: San Telmo

This tiny place is popular with locals and tourists, this small restaurant (the kitchen is in full view where you can see the owner slaving away cooking his meat-centric dishes) offers a menu with a distinct Argentine influence. Try the rabbit stew, it's a favorite.

CANTINA PIERINO
Lavalle 3499, Buenos Aires, 54 11-4864-5715
No Website
CUISINE: Italian
DRINKS: Full Bar
SERVING: Lunch, Dinner
PRICE RANGE: $$$
NEIGHBORHOOD: Almagro
If you don't want to learn the tango, the next best thing is to come to this Italian-style cantina because it's filled with loads of tango memorabilia. The food is homemade Italian cuisine. Actually, there's really not a menu, they just bring you food and everything is cooked fresh. This place is always packed.

CHAN CHAN
Hipolito Yrigoyen 1390, Buenos Aires, 54 11 4382-8492
https://chanchanbsas.business.site
CUISINE: Peruvian
DRINKS: Full bar
SERVING: Lunch & Dinner; Dinner only on Sat
PRICE RANGE: $$
NEIGHBORHOOD: Congreso
Great place to go to experience Peruvian cuisine at a budget price. People crowd in here during the lunch hour packed tight as sardines, chowing down on

plates of ceviche, ajiaco de conejo (rabbit stew), arroz chaufa (fried rice Peruvian style), Creamy Chicken and Cheese stuffed fish. My advice is to wash it all down with an excellent Peruvian beer.

CHILA
Alicia Moreau de Justo 1160, Buenos Aires, +54 11 4343-6067
www.chilaweb.com.ar
CUISINE: Modern Argentinean
DRINKS: Full bar
SERVING: Dinner; closed Mon
PRICE RANGE: $$$$
NEIGHBORHOOD: Puerto Madero
Argentinean cuisine served a la carte or from the pre-fix menu. The chef studied in
Spain, so there are some interesting twists on local dishes. Also, you can find non-traditional dishes served including: Quail, quinoa and sucking pig. Unlike a lot of restaurants here, seafood is emphasized. Nice wine selection.

CHORI
Thames 1653, Buenos Aires, +54 11 3966-9857
www.facebook.com/Xchorix/
CUISINE: Steakhouse/Argentinean
DRINKS: Full Bar
SERVING: Lunch & Dinner; closed Mondays
PRICE RANGE: $
NEIGHBORHOOD: Palermo
Perfect place for Choripan (chorizo on bread). This place treats the humble sandwich like a king, and produces a gourmet version of it. Favorites: Colorado

Picate and Smoked Pork. Great selection of artisanal beers and classic tonic drinks.

CROQUE MADAME
NATIONAL MUSEUM OF DECORATIVE ART
Av Callao 1569, Buenos Aires, 54 11 4812-0777
www.croquemadame.com.ar
CUISINE: Tea Room/Coffee Shop
DRINKS: Beer & Wine
SERVING: Lunch, Dinner
PRICE RANGE: $$$$
NEIGHBORHOOD: Palermo
Located in the Museum of Decorative Art, this

café/restaurant is a great stop for an afternoon snack or coffee after touring the museum. (I stop in the morning for café con leche before touring the museum—get the homemade scones.) It's actually out in a courtyard where you'll love the sound of the wind rustling through the tall shade trees and listen to the splashing fountains. Menu offers a variety of sandwiches, pizzas, pastas and sweet treats, and of course the signature Croques.

CUMANA
Rodriguez Pena 1149, Buenos Aires, +54 11 4813-9207
No Website
CUISINE: Argentine, Tapas/Small Plates, Pizza
DRINKS: Beer & Wine Only
SERVING: Lunch & Dinner
PRICE RANGE: $$
NEIGHBORHOOD: Recoleta
You probably haven't seen an adobe oven before, but they have one here. Large windows let the light flow in during the day. A great budget place. Taste some of the delicious authentic Argentinean (regional) cuisine including empanadas, pizzas (different that American pizza) and stews. Go for a *cazuela*, which is essentially a stew of corn, eggplant, potatoes, squash and meat. Bursting with flavor. Welcoming to tourists but it's essentially a locals' eatery.

DON JULIO
Guatemala 4691, Buenos Aires, +54 11 4831-9564
www.parrilladonjulia.com.ar
WEBSITE DOWN AT PRESSTIME
CUISINE: Steakhouse
DRINKS: Beer & Wine Only
SERVING: Lunch & Dinner
PRICE RANGE: $$$

Rustic steakhouse with a costumed maître d' greeting guests. He will seat you at a table covered with a leather tablecloth (each one the hide of a whole cow). Great place for meat lovers with an extensive wine list. Try the grilled provolone with tomato as an appetizer and you can't go wrong ordering one of their steaks. But instead of the usual sirloin, tenderloin or delicious skirt steak, I'd try their sweetbreads, delectable morsels expertly prepared. Or their kidneys and chitlins as a starter. Seating upstairs and down.

EL BAQUEANO
Chile 499, Buenos Aires, +54 11 4342-0802
www.restoelbaqueano.com
CUISINE: Argentinean
DRINKS: Full Bar
SERVING: Dinner; closed Sun & Mon
PRICE RANGE: $$$$
NEIGHBORHOOD: Monserrat

A unique restaurant as it only serves local game meat – everything from Lama to fish. Nice wine pairings. Great tasting menu.

EL FERROVIARIO
Reservistas Argentinos 219, +54 11 4644-2360
No Website
CUISINE: Argentine / steakhouse
DRINKS: Beer & Wine Only
SERVING: Lunch & Dinner
PRICE RANGE: $$
NEIGHBORHOOD: Liniers
Great menu offering everything from squid to all kinds of meat, as befitting a "popular," which is the Argentine word for steakhouse. Wonderfully rustic and charming atmosphere with clusters of garlic hanging from the wood-beamed cathedral ceiling along with sides of cured ham, cheeses, etc. Big tables are meant to seat families or a group of friends, so a crowd is welcome. (There's a tent outside for the overflow crowd.) This used to be the cafeteria for the Liniers football stadium. Favorites: parrillada, or mixed grill, which includes everything from sweetbreads, chorizo, proveleta, large cuts of succulent and aroma rich meat ready to fall from the bone. Nice selection of desserts including an incredible flan.

EL MIRASOL DAL PUERTO
Av. Alicia Moreau de Justo 202, +54 11 4315-6277
www.elmirasol.com.ar
CUISINE: Steakhouse
DRINKS: Full Bar

SERVING: Lunch & Dinner
PRICE RANGE: $$$
NEIGHBORHOOD: Puerto Madero

Nice eatery (the name of this place means "the sunflower of the port") with English speaking waiters that help you navigate the menu in this lovely spot that overlooks the sparkling yachts docked outside. Beside the quay you're surrounded by soaring office towers, but here it's very quaint for a power lunch place that attracts well-heeled business types. Favorites: just throw caution and calories to the wind and indulge in the meats on offer here—the 1.5 pound cut is ordered by more people than you'd think, but you can get a simple 1-pound steak if you like. If you order a whole chorizo, be prepared to share it. The Salmon empanadas are well worth sampling. Note: there is a minimal "per person" charge.

EL POBRE LUIS
Arribeños 2393, Buenos Aires, 11-4780-5847
CUISINE: Argentinian
DRINKS: Full Bar
SERVING: Lunch, Dinner
PRICE RANGE: $$$$
NEIGHBORHOOD: Capital Federal
A favorite restaurant among the locals for their house specialty, Pamplona – Beef, Chicken or Pork rolled with ham, cheese and red peppers and then grilled. Still, I prefer the veal sweetbreads or the ojo de bife (rib eye). This place has an open parrilla (grill), making it easy to watch the cooks slinging all that meat around. A great spectacle. (Closed Sundays).

EL PREFERIDO DE PALERMO
Jorge Luis Borges 2108, Buenos Aires, +54 11 4774-6585

No Website
CUISINE: Argentinean
DRINKS: Full Bar
SERVING: Lunch & Dinner; closed Sun
PRICE RANGE: $$
NEIGHBORHOOD: Palermo
This place looks like a small old market but it's a great choice for snacks and drinks. Not a touristy stop – locals only. Favorites: Tripe stew (a starter) and Veal ribs with salad. Most dishes are cooked home style. Don't leave without trying the flan with dulce de leche for dessert.

ELENA
Posadas 1086, Buenos Aires, +54 11 4321-1200
https://www.fourseasons.com/buenosaires
CUISINE: Argentine
DRINKS: Full bar
SERVING: Breakfast, Lunch & Dinner
PRICE RANGE: $$$$
NEIGHBORHOOD: Retiro
Chic restaurant located in the **Four Seasons Hotel**, offering fine dining experience. It's one of those places you go for a special occasion like a birthday because it's no nice, with great service and high prices. (Not that I've ever needed a reason to pamper myself!) Beautiful décor and excellent menu. Menu includes Argentinean Kobe beef, chicken, pork, and seafood. Great breakfast buffet. Seafood is fresh with large portions.

DELFIN DEL MUNDO
Honduras 5663, Buenos Aires, 54 11 4899-6660

www.bodegadelfindelmundo.com
CUISINE: Argentine
DRINKS: Full Bar
SERVING: Lunch, Dinner
PRICE RANGE: $$$$
NEIGHBORHOOD: Palermo
This trendy restaurant, with a lovely interior, offers five and six course meals with wine pairings. Here their specialty seems to be steak served several ways. Nice wine list.

FERVOR
Posadas 1519, Buenos Aires, 54 11 4804-4944
www.fervorbrasas.com.ar
CUISINE: Argentinian
DRINKS: Full Bar
SERVING: Lunch, Dinner
PRICE RANGE: $$
NEIGHBORHOOD: Recoleta
This trendy restaurant is a favorite of locals and tourists. Menu favorites include: Ojo de bife (rib-eye steak) and Tortilla de papas (fried potato omelet). The seafood is top-notch here as well.

FLORERÍA ATLÁNTICO
Arroyo 872, Buenos Aires, 54-11-4313-6093
www.floreriaatlantico.com.ar
CUISINE: Tapas; excellent cocktail selection
DRINKS: Full Bar
SERVING: Lunch, Dinner
PRICE RANGE: $$$
NEIGHBORHOOD: Retiro

This is a hot little place you just have to make time to visit. Inspired by speakeasies, it hidden beneath a flower shop. You gain entrance by passing through a huge refrigerator door and then you move downstairs. Though the food is top notch, you'll come here for the creative cocktails divided on the menu by the nationalities that inspired them: Inglaterra (for those

gin martinis), French, Italian, Polish. The subterranean cavern is decorated with paintings of fearsome sea monsters. As I said, the food is tasty: superior blood sausages (everybody freaks out when I eat these in the States), frogs' legs, octopus, beef tongue.

FLORIDA GARDEN
Florida 899, Buenos Aires, 54 11 4312-7902
No website
CUISINE: Coffee Shop
DRINKS: Full Bar
SERVING: Lunch, Dinner
PRICE RANGE: $
NEIGHBORHOOD: Capital Federal
This place is oozing with old-world charm. Great standup coffee bar for afternoon coffee, cookies, or pastries. A local's hangout and a favorite among the artsy set.

GRAN DABBANG
Av. Raúl Scalabrini Ortiz 1543, Buenos Aires, +54 11 4832-1186
www.grandabbang.com
WEBSITE DOWN AT PRESS TIME
CUISINE: Mediterranean/Indian
DRINKS: Beer & Wine Only
SERVING: Breakfast, Lunch & Dinner; closed Sun
PRICE RANGE: $$
NEIGHBORHOOD: Palermo
In this laid back dining room that's ultra casual with its wooden tables there's a creative menu of Mediterranean cuisine with an Asian/Indian flair. Favorites from the menu include the Burrata with eggplant and savory pancake, quail marinated in ginger and garlic. Vegetarian options.

I LATINA
Murillo 725, Buenos Aires, 54 11 4857-9095
www.ilatinabuenosaires.com
CUISINE: Latin American / Colombian
DRINKS: Full Bar
SERVING: Dinner
PRICE RANGE: $$$$
NEIGHBORHOOD: Villa Crespo / Palermo Queens
Two brothers and a sister from Colombia have made this one of the trendy go-to places not just in this part

of town, but all of BA. (It's certainly one of the best restaurants in town.) They have a 7-course tasting menu I'd recommend, paired with excellent Argentine wines. (The tasting menu changes with each season.) Look for the white-corn arepas with a touch of anise, accompanied by avocado and pork cracklings, or the succulent prawns caramelized in a coconut sauce and served over pineapple and fennel. Though pricey for BA, this meal would set you back 2 or 3 times the cost in the U.S.

LA BRIGADA
Estados Unidos 465, Buenos Aires, Buenos Aires, 54 11 4361–4685
www.parrillalabrigada.com.ar
WEBSITE DOWN AT PRESS TIME
CUISINE: Steakhouse
DRINKS: Full Bar
SERVING: Lunch, Dinner
PRICE RANGE: $$$$
NEIGHBORHOOD: San Telmo
The décor is a bit elaborate mixed with soccer mementos but this is one of the best parrillas in the bohemian San Telmo area. The owner chooses his own cattle from a ranch that grass feeds them. The steaks here are so tender you can eat it with a spoon. Menu favorites include: Asado (short rib roast) and Lomo (sirloin steak, prepared with a mushroom or pepper sauce). The asado de tira especial is a delicious piece of beef with the rib bones in that weighs in at 800 grams (about 28 ounces). It's almost worth the trip to B.A. by itself.

LA CABAÑA
Av Alicia Moreau de Justo 380, Buenos Aires, 54 11 4314-3710
www.lacabana.com.ar
CUISINE: Steakhouse
DRINKS: Full Bar
SERVING: Lunch, Dinner
PRICE RANGE: $$
NEIGHBORHOOD: Puerto Madero
The third incarnation of the legendary eatery, this place specializes in beef but the menu also includes chicken, fish, and a large variety of salads. You can get pieces of beef served as large as 2.2 pounds. But I'd go for the filet mignon with noisette potatoes.

LA CABRERA
Cabrera 5099, Buenos Aires, 011 4832 5754
www.lacabrera.com.ar
CUISINE: Steakhouse
DRINKS: Full Bar
SERVING: Lunch, Dinner
PRICE RANGE: $$$$
NEIGHBORHOOD: Palermo Viejo
Housed in a former general store situated in the heart of the nightlife district, you'll find an attractive crowd crammed in here well after 10 P.M., stuffing themselves before heading out for a night on the town. This eatery offers a menu that celebrates steak. You'll want to get the ribeye, naturally, a 3-inch cut

of sheer beauty, perfectly prepared. Here the portions are large and they serve delicious sweetbreads. Side dishes include pumpkin purée and eggplant salad. Get one of the Malbecs from their extensive list that will match your steak in exquisite fashion

LA CARNICERIA
2317 Thames, Buenos Aires, +54 11 2071-7199
https://www.facebook.com/xlacarniceriax
CUISINE: Argentinean/Steakhouse
DRINKS: Beer & Wine Only
SERVING: Dinner; Open for lunch Sat & Sun
PRICE RANGE: $$
Just a couple of blocks off the Avenida Santa Fe is this casual place (butcher block tables), a favorite for meat eaters, but they do offer a fish special daily. (Don't order it—stick with the meat.) The grass-fed beef served here comes from the owner's ranch in the Pampas. Get the asado de tira (smoked short ribs). Try to grab one of the handful of seats at the bar which faces the grill. Small menu and small bar selection but they are pros at preparing and serving Argentine beef. The restaurant is small and usually packed with two seatings.

LA ESPERANZA DE LOS ASCURRA
Aguirre 526, Buenos Aires, 54 11 2058-8313
No Website
CUISINE: Tapas
DRINKS: Full Bar
SERVING: Lunch, Dinner
PRICE RANGE: $$$
NEIGHBORHOOD: Villa Crespo

This popular little tapas eatery offers a creative menu. Menu favorites include: Prawns in garlic and Beef testicles (mollejas). Get away from the Malbec wine you've been drinking everywhere else and order negronis.

LA MAR, CEBICHERIA PERUANA
Arévalo 2024, Buenos Aires, +54 11 4776-5543
www.lamarcebicheria.com.ar
CUISINE: Peruvian/Seafood
DRINKS: Full Bar
SERVING: Lunch & Dinner; closed Mon
PRICE RANGE: $$
NEIGHBORHOOD: Palermo
Ceviche fans will love this elegant eatery as theirs is top notch. Also serving fresh seafood. Reservations recommended as this place books up fast. Nice cocktails.

LA RAMBLA
Posadas 1602, Buenos Aires, 54 11 4804-6958
No Website
CUISINE: Sandwiches
DRINKS: No Booze
SERVING: Lunch, Dinner
PRICE RANGE: $
NEIGHBORHOOD: Capital Federal
This extremely casual café is a sandwich place offering a great variety on their menu. Menu favorites include: Perfectly cooked steak sandwich with tomato on French bread. Delivery service available.

LAS PIZARRAS
Thames 2296, Buenos Aires, +54 11 4775-0625
www.laspizarrasbistro.com

CUISINE: Argentine
DRINKS: Full bar
SERVING: Dinner; closed Mon
PRICE RANGE: $$$
NEIGHBORHOOD: Palermo
Small "closed door" restaurant so reservations are needed. Menu favorites include: Suckling pig and Duck confit. Great choice if you're looking for something other than steak. Nice selection of desserts.

LO DE JOAQUIN DE ALBERDI
Jorge Luis Borges 1772, Buenos Aires, 54 11 4832-5329
www.lodejoaquinalberdi.com.ar
CUISINE: Wine Bar
DRINKS: Full Bar
PRICE RANGE: $$$
NEIGHBORHOOD: Palermo
Great selection of Argentine wines served at this popular wine bar. While you're tasting wines (and they'll do a personalized tasting flight for you if you like), you can snack on plates of cheese and excellent

ham. A perfect place to get away from the street after a busy day of shopping.

LOS SALONES DEL PIANO NOBILE @PARK HYATT
Av. Alvear 1661, Buenos Aires, 54 11 5171-1351
https://www.hyatt.com/en-US/hotel/argentina/palacio-duhau-park-hyatt-buenos-aires/bueph/dining
CUISINE: French
DRINKS: Full Bar
SERVING: Lunch, Dinner
PRICE RANGE: $$$$
NEIGHBORHOOD: Recoleta
Located at the Palace, this lovely restaurant serves breakfast, lunch, dinner, elegant snacks and afternoon tea. Menu favorites include: Pappardelle with Veal Ragu and Lamb Burger with fried egg and arugula.

MALVON CONFITERIA
Serrano 789, Buenos Aires, 54 11 4774-2563
www.malvonba.com.ar
CUISINE: Coffee Shop/Cafeteria
DRINKS: No Booze
SERVING: Breakfast, Lunch, Dinner
PRICE RANGE: $$
NEIGHBORHOOD: Capital Federal
This popular coffee shop/cafeteria offers an ever-changing variety of foods from around the globe. They serve all day, everything from breakfast to tapas. This place is also a bakery with a variety of sweets to eat with coffee or take home. They serve an

American style brunch with pancakes and eggs Benedict that draws huge crowds on the weekend.

MAZZO
Gurruchaga 707, Buenos Aires, 54-11 4772-8390
CUISINE: Latin American / Colombian
DRINKS: Full Bar
SERVING: Breakfast, lunch, dinner
PRICE RANGE: $$ / Cash only
NEIGHBORHOOD: Villa Crespo / Palermo Queens
In an industrial setting you sit at wooden tables or outside. Good place in this trendy area for a quick bite, but not much more.

MIRAMAR
Avenida San Juan 1999, Buenos Aires, 011 4304 4261
No Website
CUISINE: Argentinean/Spanish
DRINKS: Wine
SERVING: Lunch, Dinner
PRICE RANGE: $$$
NEIGHBORHOOD: El Centro

This restaurant serves typical Spanish fare. Menu offers dishes like Tortillas, Rabbita and Frog Legs. Well stocked wine cellar.

MIRANDA PARILLA
Costa Rica 5602, Buenos Aires, +54 11 4771-4255
www.parrillamiranda.com
CUISINE: Steakhouse/Argentinean
DRINKS: Full bar

SERVING: Breakfast, Lunch & Dinner
PRICE RANGE: $$$
NEIGHBORHOOD: Palermo
A great choice for meat lovers. Go either for the ribe eye or the grilled short ribs. They serve a variety of cuts and local pastas like the Spinach and Ricotta Raviolis with cream sauce. Nice wine selection of big rich Cabernets to go with the meats. (Or choose from a great selection of Malbecs.)

MISHIGUENE
Lafinur 3368, Buenos Aires, +54 11 3969-0764
www.mishiguene.com
CUISINE: Middle Eastern
DRINKS: Full bar
SERVING: Lunch & Dinner; Lunch only on Sun
PRICE RANGE: $$$
NEIGHBORHOOD: Palermo
It's generated a lot of buzz since it opened late in 2014. Always busy, has a great energy. It's a beautiful eatery with a menu of Middle Eastern cuisine (including some modern Jewish food, something rare in these parts) with an Argentinean twist. Dishes served are large portions perfect for sharing. Menu favorites include: Varenikes and Humas.
Impressive wine list.

NOLA
Gorriti 4389, Buenos Aires, +54 9 11 5760-6652
www.nolabuenosaires.com
CUISINE: Cajun/Creole

DRINKS: Full bar
SERVING: Dinner
PRICE RANGE: $$
NEIGHBORHOOD: Palermo

Who would have thought you'd find a gastro pub in Buenos Aires specializing in food from New Orleans? New Orleans favorites like gumbo, buttermilk battered fried chicken and sweetbreads are served. Crafted beers and nice selection of wines. Very informal dining with a "fast food" feeling.

NUCHA CAFE
Jerónimo Salguero 2587, Buenos Aires, 54 11 4808-0179
www.nucha.com.ar
CUISINE: Argentinean/Confection Shop
DRINKS: No Booze
SERVING: Breakfast
PRICE RANGE: $
NEIGHBORHOOD: Palermo

This confection shop offers a great selection of pastries and cakes to enjoy with coffee or tea (nice variety). It's all made here on the premises. (They even make their own chocolates.) Get the tortas favi, which is layer cake with chocolate mousse & cream crowned by a slab of light-as-air Italian meringue. The chocolate truffles aren't bad, either.

NUESTRO SECRETO
Cerrito 1455, Buenos Aires, 54-11-4321-1552
www.fourseasons.com/buenosaires/dining/restaurants/nuestro_secreto/
CUISINE: Argentinean/BBQ
DRINKS: Full bar
SERVING: Lunch & Dinner; closed Mon & Tues
PRICE RANGE: $$$
NEIGHBORHOOD: Retiro
Located at the **Four Seasons Hotel**, this unique eatery serves up a "backyard garden" atmosphere

complete with outdoor furniture overlooking the pool. It's a very relaxing place, with glass walls and even a glass roof. Cuisine is typical Argentinean with a great selection of meats with a focus on BBQ. (But the best choices are those cuts smoked using different hardwoods native to the country.)

OCHO ONCE
El Salvador y Ravignani, Palermo, Buenos Aires, 15 3614-5719
www.facebook.com/ochooncemaison/#_=_
CUISINE: Steakhouse/BBQ
DRINKS: Full Bar
SERVING: Dinner – Wed – Sat
PRICE RANGE: $$$$
Like most closed door restaurants (reservations a must) you will only find out about this place by word of mouth. (I'm your word-of-mouth guy.) Located in a renovated house, this small eatery offers a warm ambiance and a delicious menu from a great chef. The restaurant serves only organic 100% certified Argentinian beef in a 5 course tasting menu – changing weekly. Meats prevail but nice fish options and delicious homemade bread. Fried cheese, quinoa burgers, mushroom paté are among the tapas offered. (Don't show up too early. Doesn't get busy till 11 or even midnight.)

OSAKA
Soler 5608, Buenos Aires, 54 11 4775–6964
www.osaka.com.pe
CUISINE: Japanese Fusion
DRINKS: Full Bar

SERVING: Lunch, Dinner
PRICE RANGE: $$$$
NEIGHBORHOOD: Palermo
This innovative restaurant blends Peruvian and Asian cuisines to the delight of their well-dressed young hip guests who keep the place packed. Menu favorite: Misoudado, an amazing red-curry grouper. Upstairs and downstairs dining.

OVIEDO
Antonio Beruti 2602, Buenos Aires, 54 11 4822-5415
www.oviedoresto.com.ar
CUISINE: Argentinean/Spanish
DRINKS: Full Bar
SERVING: Lunch, Dinner
PRICE RANGE: $$$$
NEIGHBORHOOD: Capital Federal/ Recoleta
This very upscale Spanish-style restaurant offers a menu that includes everything from classics to new and modern creations. Excellent cheeses. Daily fish

specials are a favorite but their meats are primo as well. Impressive wine list.

PALADAR
Camargo, Buenos Aires, +54 9 11 5797-7267
www.paladarbuenosaires.com.ar
CUISINE: Signature Cuisine (well, they said it, not me)
DRINKS: Full Bar
SERVING: Dinner & Late Night
PRICE RANGE: $$$$

With quite a few options to the "closed door" scene in Buenos Aires, this is a lovely choice where reservations are made online and they send you the address. Creative menu is most filled with traditional but innovative Argentinian dishes. The owners speak English and welcome all for a lovely dining experience.

PARRILLA DON JULIO
Guatemala 4691, Buenos Aires, +54 11 4831-9564
www.parrilladonjulio.com.ar
CUISINE: Steakhouse
DRINKS: Full Bar
SERVING: Lunch & Dinner
PRICE RANGE: $$
NEIGHBORHOOD: Palermo

Popular steakhouse serving classic steaks and local dishes. Menu picks: Rib Eye (from grass-fed cattle) and Flan (for dessert). Upscale dining with perfect service – don't go here if you're in a rush. Nice wine selection.

PATAGONIA SUR
Rocha 801, Buenos Aires, 54 11 4303-5917
www.restaurantepatagoniasur.com
CUISINE: Argentinean
DRINKS: Full Bar
SERVING: Lunch, Dinner
PRICE RANGE: $$$$
NEIGHBORHOOD: Boca/Capital Federal
Run by Francis Mallman, chef and author, who offers an impressive menu of Argentinean fare that showcases local produce. Menu favorites include: 7 hour Lamb and Beef tenderloin with bacon. Very impressive wine cellar. Reservations necessary.

PROPER
Aráoz 1676, Buenos Aires, +54 11 4831-0027
www.properbsas.com.ar
CUISINE: Argentinean
DRINKS: Full Bar
SERVING: Dinner; closed Sun & Mon

PRICE RANGE: $$
NEIGHBORHOOD: Palermo
Located on a small side street, the door is usually closed but knock and you'll be welcomed. Mostly locals. Cuisine is authentic Argentinean with a variety of seasonal tapas and steaks. Nice wine pairings. Like most Argentinean eateries, here the flan is one of their specialties.

RODI BAR
Vincente Lopez 1900, Buenos Aires, +54 11 4801-5230
No Website
CUISINE: Peruvian
DRINKS: Beer & Wine Only
SERVING: Lunch & Dinner; closed Sun
PRICE RANGE: $$$
NEIGHBORHOOD: Recoleta
Intimate (yes, the tables are that close together) high-end eatery with a loyal following. This place has long been an institution in the wealthy Recoleta district, but the food is simple and unpretentious. A good place to get a cheap combination plate. Menu favorites include: Veal cutlet with fried egg and Spinach crepes. Reservations recommended.

SALGADO ALIMENTOS
Juan Ramírez de Velazco 401, Buenos Aires, 54 11 4854-1336
www.salgadoalimentos.com.ar/
WEBSITE DOWN AT PRESS TIME
CUISINE: Italian/Pasta
DRINKS: Full Bar

SERVING: Lunch, Dinner
PRICE RANGE: $
NEIGHBORHOOD: Villa Crespo / Palermo Queens
This popular Italian eatery offers a menu with a variety of homemade pastas and sauces. Unlike some of the trendier new arrivals to this recently hot area, this place has been around for many years. Try the

Pumpkin Ravioli or the pork shoulder ravioli. An old favorite here is the "provoleta," or grilled provolone. Just add a little salt and you're in heaven. Outdoor seating. Delivery available.

TEGUI
Costa Rica 5852, Buenos Aires, 54 11 4770 9500
www.tegui.com.ar
CUISINE: Eclectic
DRINKS: Full Bar
SERVING: Lunch, Dinner
PRICE RANGE: $$$$

NEIGHBORHOOD: Palermo
Local culinary bigwig German Martitegue opened

Tegui in 2009 and has been serving crowds ever since. Very stylish eatery with an open-air kitchen in the rear. (You go through a large display of wine bottles up front, then pass through an atrium with palm trees, before getting to the rear.) Very handsome staff, right out of some modeling agency. The menu is prix-fixe with four choices for starters, entrees, and desserts. Menu favorites include: Cow-brain pie with prosciutto and shallot cream sauce and Rabbit-stuffed ravioli. But menu changes every week. Extensive wine list. I'd advise reservations. Restaurant magazine dubbed this the 9th best restaurant among the top 50 in all of Latin America.

TOMO 1

Carlos Pellegrini 521, Buenos Aires, +54 11 4326 6695

www.tomo1.com.ar

CUISINE: Argentine / Spanish / Italian
DRINKS: Full bar
SERVING: Lunch & Dinner; closed Sun
PRICE RANGE: $$$$
NEIGHBORHOOD: San Nicolas

Located in the **Panamericano Buenos Aires Hotel & Resort**, this is a formal upscale eatery with white tablecloths and exquisite service to match. A good idea here is to get the 3-course tasting menu. Price includes 2 glasses of wine, coffee and dessert, so in a place like this, it's a bargain. . Menu favorites include: Patagonia lamb gigot and the delicious dessert crème brûlée trio (combination of vanilla, dulce de leche and coffee). Reservations recommended.

UCO
Soler 5862, Buenos Aires, +54 11 3220-6820
www.fierrohotel.com
CUISINE: Argentinean
DRINKS: Full Bar
SERVING: Breakfast, Lunch & Dinner
PRICE RANGE: $$
NEIGHBORHOOD: Palermo Hollywood
Located in **Hotel Fierro** is this hip eatery helmed by a talented chef who offers a menu of fresh, farm-to-kitchen cuisine. It's got a great look that makes you feel like you're in some barn out in the country. Wood paneled walls, leather banquettes. Menu includes variety of items all prepared in-house like ice-creams, patés, breads, chutneys, cured bacon and smoked trout. Choose from the 7 course tasting menu

or order a la carte. Hopefully, the night you're there they'll have my favorite, the roasted Patagonian lamb shoulder (serves 2 or even 3 persons). Slow cooked for 12 hours. Impressive wine list. Try the tasty apple tart with dulce de leche.

NIGHTLIFE

DID YOU FIND AN INTERESTING PLACE?
If you discover a place you think I should check out on my next visit, drop me a line, will you? I'll mention your name if I end up listing it.
andrewdelaplaine@mac.com

BEBOP CLUB
Moreno 364, Buenos Aires, +54 11 4331-3409
www.bebopclub.com.ar
NEIGHBORHHOOD: Monserrat
Reminiscent of a swanky New York jazz club. Downstairs is the club; upstairs is a nice restaurant with an extensive wine list, **Aldo's Restoran Vinoteca**. There's a drink minimum in the club

portion. Jazz & Blues. International as well as local music acts featured. Closed Mondays.

EL BOLICHE DE ROBERTO
2280 Blanca Encalada, Buenos Aires, +54 11 6937-5356
NEIGHBORHHOOD: Belgrano
Fun dive bar with cheap wine. Live music and a great place to hear tango music without having to dance to it. The band strikes up around 10:30. Crowds sometimes overflow into the street. A very authentic Argentinean scene – very little English is spoken here.

THE HARRISON SPEAKEASY
Palermo Soho
C1414DMJ, Malabia 1764, Buenos Aires, 54 11 4831 0519
The "closed door" concept is popular in Buenos Aires and they have many "speakeasy" themed bars. To gain entrance to this bar you need to have friends that have a membership card or have dinner at **Nicky's**

NY sushi bar and when you finish dinner ask to visit the wine cellar. You'll be sent through a door in the rear of the place that looks like a vault. Once inside, it's a great bar scene and it really feels like you're in a New York bar in the 1920s, with the big wooden bar and the sparkling crystal chandeliers.

ISABEL BAR
Uriarte 1664 Ciudad Autonoma, Buenos Aires, 54-11 4834-6969
www.isabelbar.com
NEIGHBORHOOD: Palermo Soho
Open since 2010, this trendy bar became famous as the place to spot models. Drinks are purchased with Isabelitas, 25-peso poker chips purchased upon entering the club. The bar has a funky classic décor with an outside patio.

LA CATEDRAL
Sarmiento 4006, Buenos Aires, 54 11 5325 1630

www.lacatedralclub.com/
NEIGHBORHOOD: Almagro
This underground club is a mixture of post-punk/neo-goth and circus/music hall. Great tango experience for watching and learning the dance. The regulars here often invite strangers to dance the tango, so you can learn a few steps. Cover charge.

LA PLAYITA
Roseti 722, Buenos Aires
www.agrupacionlaplayita.blogspot.com.ar
NEIGHBORHOOD: Chacarita
You have to ring a doorbell to get into this old reconditioned house that sports a patio and bar where concerts are put on by a variety of performers. On busy nights, a line forms. You pay a cheap cover and then you're in a world of cast-off sofas, mismatched chairs, cheap local beers that are cold and delicious and a underground scene.

LA TRASTIENDA CLUB
Balcarce 460 San Telmo, Buenos Aires, 54 11 4342-5162
www.latrastienda.com
NEIGHBORHOOD: San Telmo
Translated as The Hidden, this club is located in the historic district in a building that was once an old general store. This place is a landmark in the cultural scene of the city. Here all styles of music are performed including Pop, Rock, Reggae, Electronic, World, Tango, Jazz and Folklore.

LA VIRUTA
Armenia 1366, Buenos Aires, +54 11 5263 0964
www.lavirutatango.com
NEIGHBORHOOD: Palermo Soho
One of the most popular dance venues in Buenos Aires that is also know for the dance classes scheduled every day and night. If you pay once, you can attend as many classes as you want during that day. Tango rules here and the slippery dance floor is ideal. Tables are available if you just want to drink and watch (which is where I personally fit in). Live music. This place gets packed around 3 a.m. and is open until dawn. (How these people do it, I don't know. You and old, they're all up late.)

SHOUT BRASAS & DRINKS
Maipú 981, Buenos Aires, +54 11 4313-2850
www.shoutbar.com.ar
NEIGHBORHHOOD: Retiro / Microcentro
Located in a beautiful mansion, this mazelike bar serves great cocktails. Food is also good but this is a

favorite stop for cocktails. Very knowledgeable about Argentinean wine. Reservations recommended. Cocktail menus in Spanish only but there are a few English speakers on staff.

TEATRO COLÓN
Cerrito 628, Buenos Aires, 54 11 4378-7100
www.teatrocolon.org.ar
NEIGHBORHOOD: Capital Federal
Open since 1908, this is the main opera house in the city and the third best opera house in the world (according to National Geographic). After a refurbishment the venue reopened in 2010.

TORQUATO TASSO
Defensa 1575 San Telmo, Buenos Aires, 54 4307 6506
www.torquatotasso.com.ar
NEIGHBORHOOD: Capital Federal

This is one of the city's best live-music venues and especially a great place to hear live tango music. Popular bands that regularly play here include: Orchestra Típica Leopoldo Federico, Sexteto Mayor and La Chicana. Cover charge.

VERNE COCKTAIL CLUB
Av. Medrano 1475, Buenos Aires, +54 11 4822-0980
www.vernecocktailclub.com
NEIGHBORHHOOD: Palermo
This place stands out among the other "speakeasy" style bars in Buenos Aires. This offers the most authentic speakeasy experience. Reservations recommended. Try the Opium Old Fashioned (made with Jim Beam) – it's a winner but all the cocktails are top notch.

VICTORIA BROWN
Costa Rica 4827, Buenos Aires, 54 11 4831-0831
www.victoriabrownbar.com
NEIGHBORHOOD: Palermo
In jaded upscale Palermo, this place has got people buzzing like schoolchildren. In the daytime, it's known for putting out a superior brunch menu. But when the sun goes down, the phony brick wall slides open revealing a plush speakeasy bar entered through a secret passage. The craft cocktails really involve some craft. The Desde Cuba con Amor comes out literally smoking. Once you're inside, the mood is friendly. Interesting bar menu featuring treats like octopus and spicy French toast.

INDEX

A

ACONCAGUA, 13
Aldo's Restoran Vinoteca., 57
ALDO'S VINOTECA, 13
ARAMBURU, 14
Aramburu Bis, 14
Argentine, 22, 27, 38
Argentinean, 13, 35, 41, 44, 53
Argentinian, 14

B

BBQ, 44, 45
BEBOP CLUB, 57
BOULEVARD SAENZ PENA, 15

C

CAFÉ LA BIELA, 16
CAFÉ SAN JUAN, 18
Cajun, 42
CANTINA PIERINO, 19
CASA FELIX, 17
CHAN CHAN, 19
CHILA, 20
CHORI, 20
Creole, 42
CROQUE MADAME, 21
CUMANA, 22

D

DELFIN DEL MUNDO, 27
DON JULIO, 22

E

EL BAQUEANO, 23
EL BOLICHE DE ROBERTO, 58
EL FERROVIARIO, 24
EL MIRASOL DAL PUERTO, 24
EL POBRE LUIS, 26
EL PREFERIDO DE PALERMO, 26
ELENA, 27

F

FERVOR, 28
FLORERÍA ATLÁNTICO, 28
FLORIDA GARDEN, 30
Four Seasons Hotel, 27, 44

G

GRAN DABBANG, 30

H

HARRISON SPEAKEASY, 58
Hotel Fierro, 53

I

I LATINA, 31
Indian, 30
International, 14
ISABEL BAR, 59
Italian, 24

L

LA BRIGADA, 32
LA CABANA, 33
LA CABRERA, 34
LA CARNICERIA, 35
LA CATEDRAL, 59
LA ESPERANZA DE LOS ASCURRA, 35
LA MAR, 36
LA PLAYITA, 60
LA RAMBLA, 37
LA TRASTIENDA CLUB, 60
LA VIRUTA, 61
LAS PIZARRAS, 37
LO DE JOAQUIN DE ALBERDI, 38
LOS SALONES DEL PIANO NOBILE, 39

M

MALVON CONFITERIA, 39
MAZZO, 40
Mediterranean, 30
MIRAMAR, 40
MIRANDA PARILLA, 41
MISHIGUENE, 42
Modern Argentinean, 20
Moreno Hotel, 14
MUSEUM OF DECORATIVE ART, 21

N

NOLA, 42
NUCHA CAFE, 43
NUESTRO SECRETO, 44

O

OCHO ONCE, 45
OSAKA, 45
OVIEDO, 46

P

Panamericano Buenos Aires Hotel & Resort, 52
PARK HYATT, 39
PARRILLA DON JULIO, 47
PATAGONIA SUR, 48
Peruvian, 19, 42, 49
Pizza, 22
PROPER, 48
Puertas Cerradas, 12

R

RODI BAR, 49

S

SALGADO ALIMENTOS, 49
SHOUT BRASAS & DRINKS, 61
Steakhouse, 22, 35, 41, 45

T

Tapas/Small Plates, 22

TEATRO COLÓN, 62
TEGUI, 50
TOMO 1, 52
TORQUATO TASSO, 62

U

UCO, 53

V

VERNE COCKTAIL CLUB, 63
VICTORIA BROWN, 63

WANT 3 FREE THRILLERS?

Why, of course you do!
If you like these writers--
Vince Flynn, Brad Thor, Tom Clancy, James Patterson, David Baldacci, John Grisham, Brad Meltzer, Daniel Silva, Don DeLillo
If you like these TV series –
House of Cards, Scandal, West Wing, The Good Wife, Madam Secretary, Designated Survivor

> You'll love the **unputdownable** series about Jack Houston St. Clair, with political intrigue, romance, and loads of action and suspense.

Besides writing travel books, I've written political thrillers for many years that have delighted hundreds of thousands of readers. I want to introduce you to my work!
Send me an email and I'll send you a link where you can

download the first 3 books in my bestselling series, absolutely FREE.

Mention **<u>this book</u>** when you email me.
andrewdelaplaine@mac.com